Presented to:

Never Forget The Difference You've Made

Made in the USA
Las Vegas, NV
16 August 2024

93945305R10066